Do not consistently and constantly hide your failures/insecurities in shame

DO not bad talk them when they UNDERESTIMATE YOU.

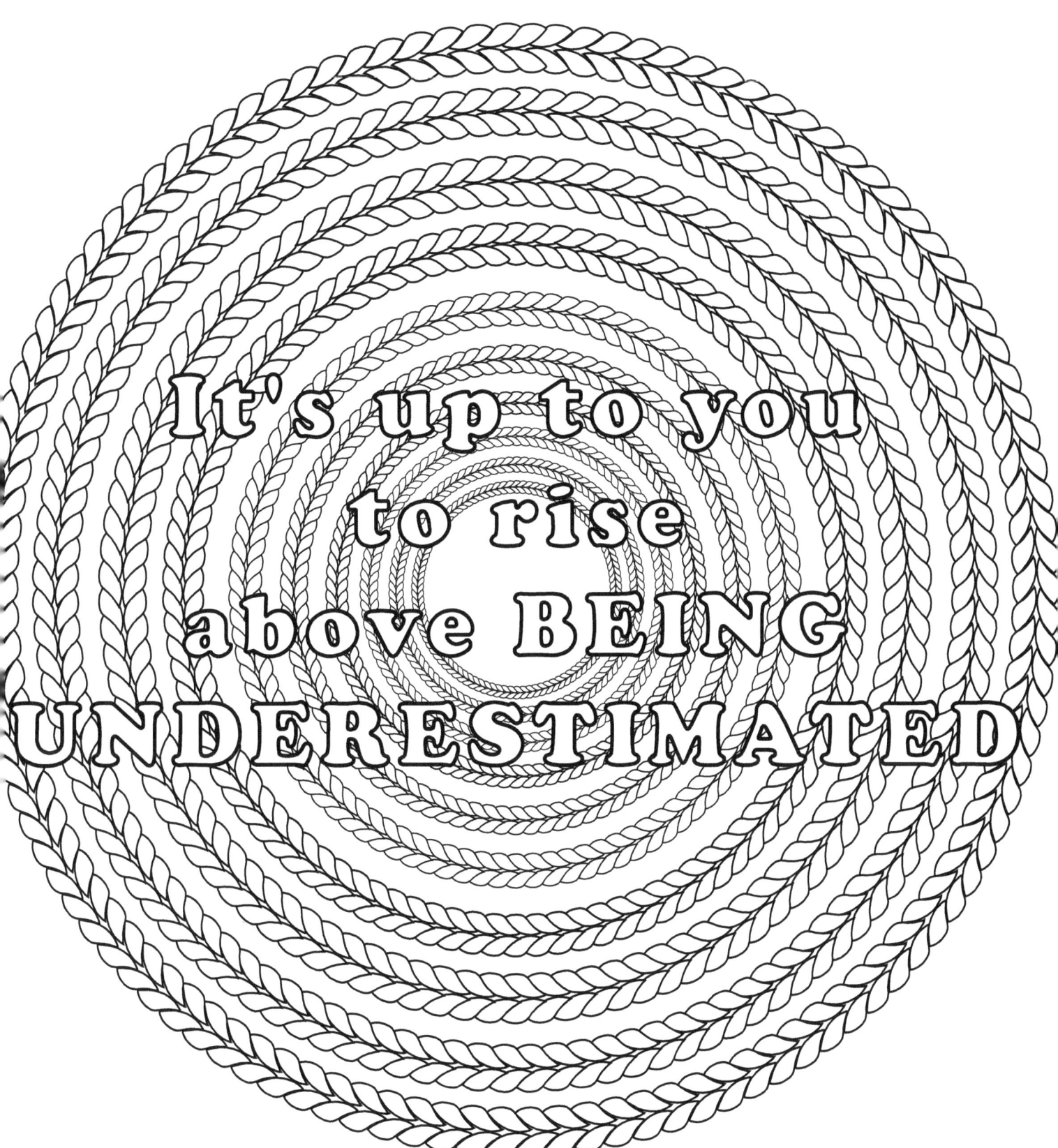

Out of those hard moments came the brilliant ladies you see before you now.

Owning your failures and forgiving yourself is key

It's hard to be known by the OBSTACLES in our lives

EXPRESSING WHAT'S BEEN BOTHERING YOU SHOULD BE NATURAL

Mess ups are a new chance to be still and regroup

We are human!! Messing up is Expected!

"1 "F" up" or multiple is a temporary setback

Launch that business & register that trademark

I remember being disappointed in myself

www.ingramcontent.com/pod-product-compliance
Lightning Source LLC
Chambersburg PA
CBHW081253040426
42453CB00014B/2399